God Drops In

Other books by Dale L. Bates

My Journey

God Drops: Wisdom to Live By

God Drops In

ENJOYING THE PRESENCE OF GOD

D A L E   L .   B A T E S

ARCHWAY
PUBLISHING

Archway Publishing books may be ordered through booksellers or by contacting:

Archway Publishing
1663 Liberty Drive
Bloomington, IN 47403
www.archwaypublishing.com
1-(888)-242-5904

ISBN: 978-1-4808-1189-8 (sc)
ISBN: 978-1-4808-1188-1 (e)

Library of Congress Control Number: 2014917962

Printed in the United States of America.

Archway Publishing rev. date: 10/30/2014

This book is dedicated to the life and writings
of Brother Lawrence.

Contents

Acknowledgments

OUR SPECIES WOULD BE TOTALLY MUTE IF OUR SPOKEN LANGUAGE WERE AS difficult as the written language is. I never paid any attention throughout my education to any grammar classes; now I could kick myself. When I finish any written page, it is chaos at best and takes a person (in my case, a couple of ladies), who did pay attention in class to finish it. I never, to my knowledge, had a mixed metaphor run over me; a dangling participle may have hit me in the right eye once, which instantly turned my eye jet black. When I get my work edited, it comes back with all those squiggly marks on everything—like periods, commas, and questions marks. Thanks to the girls.

With my work in question, I can't thank Kay Bates and Laura Behrens enough for their work ethic and hours of labor. Their interest in making this book correct, without losing me in the process, is a perfect compliment for them. Their questions and ideas really helped with the rewrites. I can honestly say that without them, this book would never have happened.

I say thanks to John DeFoore, a gifted counselor and long-time friend, for working with me for these many years and seeing to it that I had enough desire and mind to write this book. Today his mind and mine have a lot in common.

I have just finished reading a book titled *The Circle Maker: Praying Circles Around Your Biggest Dreams and Greatest Fears* by Mark Batterson. *God Drops In* was finished; but not printed, before I read *The Circle Maker,* and it occurred to me both books were about living the Presence of God. Dear reader, you might really enjoy Mark's book; it certainly changed my approach to prayer and is a fabulous book.

Prologue

This book is written for all people who live a life they know is not complete:

Anyone who spends time thinking, *I am missing something, but what?*

Anyone looking around the next corner for something and not knowing what that something is.

Anyone who has that nagging feeling in the stomach saying, "I am not living my life correctly."

Anyone who is semi-depressed for no reason.

Anyone who is not happy where he is and always wants to be somewhere else.

All those people who would never admit it, but know there is a giant hole in their life, and they have no idea how to fill it.

THIS PRESENT MOMENT IS ALL I HAVE.

The statement above is true, and it has always been true since the moment of my conception. My mother and father did not know if I would live a minute or one hundred years. As my mother held and looked at me, I doubt very much if she realized what she and God had just done.

With His help, she carried me to term, and they, together, gave me the greatest gift I would ever receive: life. Almost everything I would ever need has been given to me free of charge: a heart, and lungs that worked immediately, and all the other organs I would need to come online as needed. I also got all the air and water I could use, with no charge. My mother had to nurse and love me, and my father needed to love me and provide the money for food as I grew. Until I was about twelve years old, I never invested a dime or any thought in my life. I, like all kids, played, hung out, and like a blotter, absorbed everything I saw and was told, and then I saved it into memory.

I am quite aware that not all children born on this planet received all that I did. But I do believe most of us in America did. However, this book is primarily about the only person I know anything at all about—me.

I not only came out of the womb alive and healthy but with the acquired history and DNA from all my ancestors, covering thousands of years of their learned experiences. Almost all, if not all, of this data was stored in what I believe was my brain and generally related to rules for living—the basic instincts that all animals seem to hit the ground knowing.

I have assisted many cows and ewes in delivering their babes, and, within minutes after their birth, the mothers have them clean and are waiting for the little animals to start getting up on their own. Soon the offspring find their mother and nurse. Before you would think possible, they both walk off together, the little ones following just behind.

As I would stand there watching, I always thought, *This is just like us.* There is something in animals and in us that tells each of us what we are to do before our mothers could possibly teach us. So, on a perfect timetable, I started walking and talking, with a great deal of help from my parents and other relatives, but I had to initiate the action.

As my life progressed and I started to think for myself, I decided everything was mine. My parents knew all babies are born totally selfish, but they didn't have to explain this to me. I *was* selfish! Soon, I started daydreaming. If I didn't like something that was going on, I just left by turning my mind free to take me anyplace except where I was. This method of self-protection, selfish as it was, became my life and my copout. A new thought pattern appeared, telling me that we see and hear everything through filters. So early on, I started my "me" period. With this filter, I grew up not doing anything I didn't like doing. If I heard anything different than I wanted to hear, an instant daydream would take its place.

This daydreaming was a form of self-preservation, but it turned into a dark enterprise quickly. Soon my daydreams served to aggrandize me and destroy others who had dared to disagree with me. I got to the point that I began to see the daydream as real and reality as fantasy. Dreams also took the joy I should have felt with most honors and reduced them to a "Well, that's that" attitude because they didn't seem to have any meaning. Because I had exchanged my early life, which in most cases I did not like, for fantasy, I was not living any experiences at the level they deserved. Therefore, when anything went wrong, I could back away as if I had never been there. As I got older, I began to have many honors and some degree of acclaim, which kept me from running straight out of life and into never-never land.

Now all these years later, I see what I had really done. I did not like the first part of my life, so I changed the present into whatever experience I thought I needed. I became addicted to validation, so I began to think that what was good in small quantities should be better in larger doses—don't you agree? But this mental approach was killing me. My body shut down and became immobile. I had been running three miles each day since getting out of the military; then one of those nights, I passed out after running. I could not speak but could hear the doctor from across the alley asking me many questions; he thought I had suffered a heart attack. All my mind could focus on was Kay and both of our children. I did not think of my perfect job, my bank account, my church, or any of my many friends—only my family was important. I had to change.

My family and I moved to the farm, and I became a man of the land. Nothing could have been more therapeutic for me than agriculture. To a farmer, there is no gray area; it is either black or white. A cow is a good cow or a bad cow, no discussion. A year is a good year or a bad year, no discussion. A man is a good man or a bad man, no discussion. In a world where animals are nurtured to be slaughtered for food, or crops are harvested in order to make blue jeans, there is little room for make-believe. I, therefore, could find few places to lie to myself. A profit was very hard to make, and I did everything I knew to make a living. Gone were the daydreams; they had to be replaced with staying alive. Operating machines that weighed thousands of pounds, with all their parts moving, required all of my mental focus to stay where I was supposed to be and not fall into the moving parts.

Before I went to the farm, I had been denying the existence of the *present* so that I never had to deal with adversity; I had been daydreaming. At about thirty-five years of age, I began to hear in my mind, *Check the present*. This thought came on softly first, and as the years passed, it got louder. Say what? Who cares about the present? I had lived my life excluding the present; what could it do for me?

At that point, I had spent twenty years reading everything spiritual I could find and trying to pray, but I had no real God to pray to. That's not true; I had a God but not a history or connection with Him. I had humbled myself on the floor, read, and, I thought, studied the Bible, but little spiritual progress was happening for me. Then I discovered staying in the Presence of God, which sounded very easy, but I was still searching. I had been searching all my life, but none of the satisfaction received from honors or accolades lasted more than an hour at most. Then I would be back on a crooked, endless road searching for something, but what?

My preoccupation with making a living and constantly entertaining myself absorbed all my time and talent. Everyone I knew lived exactly the same way I did—working all the time, with no quiet time, no time for anything spiritual, except for two hours on Sunday. The laughter we generated may have been hollow laughter, but it kept us sane and—we thought—happy.

I had always been able to do more than one thing at a time, which just added to the boiling pot. My wife, Kay, had never been happy with my lifestyle but, through time, accepted it as normal. Now "normal" is a good word, but what does it mean? Webster's Dictionary says normal is "conforming to a standard, or free from a mental disorder." As anyone can see, I was normal; but I am not sure about not having the mental disorder. Yes, I could have passed a sanity test, but I was anything but happy.

When I made money, it seemed not to matter, but when I lost

money, I would go into weeks of depression. As I drove myself to succeed, some force seemed to be pushing me, but I felt no relief when I succeeded. Even with my busy-ness and distractions, nothing except Kay and the children satisfied me. It never occurred to me to stop the search for a relationship with God, *thank God*.

I had been a runner since a very young age, and I am sure I ran for the runner's high. In that high, for just a short time, I would feel the purpose for my being here, a feeling that I was one with more than just myself—with a love and peace that I knew I could never live happily without.

At this point, I got the Presence and present mixed up; I thought they were probably about the same. Nothing could have been more wrong. I would never achieve living in the Presence of God until I learned how to live in the present.

Then I learned why I had been so obsessed with God's being beyond time.

If God were infinite and eternal to me, He would have to be beyond time. What did that mean? Well, to me, it meant He lived only in the present. The present was what I had feared most. Bad people would be there! Therefore, I would do anything to avoid being in the present. Hand fighting the boogieman would be easier than being in the present moment.

With both hands shaking and a knot in my gut, I decided if God were in the present, I too was going to the same place. When I was alone, I worked for some time on how to get to the present minute, and then I discovered the present minute was not the present *minute* but the present *millisecond*.

I had made this experience of the present very difficult to obtain. It took more time than I thought it would, but the first time I got absolutely into the present, that experience was the end of my search. Nothing else could have been that wonderful! The love made me cry as peace totally overcame me. I have been there many times since, but nothing will ever come close to that first time. After all this time of my being in the way, I finally got out of the way and claimed my life as it was meant to be.

I believe I found why it was the shepherds who first discovered Jesus on Christmas night. They were the only people who had the time to hunt for Him. Now that I was a part-time shepherd, it was essential for me to have alone time. Our culture has moved so far away from alone time that it frightens us. We seem to have something stuck in both ears, or we are concentrating on some type of screen all the time. So most of us have traded daydreams for something else that keeps us from being alone and in the present. Without alone time, I would never have discovered my personal God. This may be the reason the Bible tells us that few will find the Way.

I need to say I worked with the Lord Jesus in getting to the right place. For the purposes of this book, I was led to use God's name, but it was Christ that I spent time with. In my "country mind," the two of them are the same being, sharing an office but doing different work. As either One does anything, they Both know about it.

As far as I could tell, another reason being one with the Presence of God took so long was that no one had ever written or talked to me about the Presence of God. Not one word about the Presence stuck in my mind. For this reason I will give all the credit to Brother Lawrence, a sixteenth-century French monk. Without his letters, I would still be searching all by myself. The Presence changed Brother Lawrence in every way, as it is changing me.

My world has become much safer. The sky is a stronger blue, and the earth is cleaner and friendlier. People have become so much dearer and smarter. My heart rate has slowed down, and my body doesn't hurt so much. I have now begun to realize that I am eternal, so time no longer matters. What a thought! I never have to look at another clock because time has stopped, and I am with my Lord.

I do have to watch for the selfishness I had before because it does come back. However, with my guard up and my staying in the Presence, I can handle anything. When I am there in the Presence, I do not have a single concern.

It would be so easy to place all the blame on our way of life, but that is totally unfair. We can become one with the Presence, no matter our job or condition. Brother Lawrence achieved the Presence of God while working in a very noisy and hot kitchen, feeding the local monastery. With some work and the desire, the Presence will lead anyone to Him. After all, I think that is why we are here. I think the Presence requests our constant companionship. This relationship is worth more than all our assets together. It may be that we were put here in training for eternity. So let's get started.

When I first started trying to become one with the Presence of God, my mind was almost totally filled with clutter that was getting in my way. I came to realize that most of it was the evil that had moved in there because I was not cleaning my mind as well as I cleaned my house. A broom or mop would not help me here, but what I did find was a command for the clutter to leave in the name of Christ, which worked. Almost immediately, it was gone, but the clutter would come back at first; therefore, I think we may need to try to search for the Presence over and over again.

We have to center ourselves, dear reader, in the present. It is not easy at first, so we must persevere. We must be totally quiet and cull all thoughts except for repeating over and over again, "I am in the present moment." Then we can move on to the present millisecond, and another closer step commences. Now we wait for a feeling of peace. When it comes, we ask to be one with the Presence and thank the Lord Jesus for being one with us. We do this until the wave of love and peace flows over us. Now we can just enjoy our first time ever with God Himself.

In my personal experience, the Presence stays somewhat constant, like it is giving me time off to be a husband, employee, father, friend, and brother. All I have to do now is center in the present, and He is there. I have come to believe the system was set up with Him always in the present, because that puts Him totally and always with you and with me. He is with us but does not demand *all* our attention, so we have to learn how to stay in the present in order to be with Him. Is it not wonderful that when He opens the door, it will always be open if we initiate the meeting?

God and Man

Up until now I have covered what role I have
in the Presence; now let's look at God's role.

THE SIZE OF GOD IS COMPLETELY IMPOSSIBLE FOR ME TO COMPREHEND. However, if I believe that our universe is infinite, and I do, then I can extrapolate the universe and God being one and infinite. So we have an infinite God being an infinite universe, with our living on a very small planet located on the outside of one galaxy. The universe may or may not be eternal, but God is. It appears that we were placed out of the way on our small planet; however, if all is infinite, any place in the universe would be the center [Stephen Hawking, *A Brief History of Time* (New York: Bantam Books, 1998)]. So we may not have been stuck off in a corner out of the way, after all, but jammed up in the middle where everything is happening.

God creates all things and gives control of these things away. This is just another way to say He gave us free will. With linear reasoning, we could assume we also may have some infinite parts, or soul, and total control over our life and being. We were given what is a "supreme gift" at birth, an opportunity to have a one-on-one association with God. This gift has always surrounded us, but the condition is we have to *ask* for the first meeting and work with the Divine in establishing the nature and depth of our relationship.

The total control was given to us as a blessing, but it can be abused. When we are acting out our life devoid of Him, we are working in the absence of God, and bad things usually occur. I lived a big part of my life for myself only. All actions were done for my glorification only. My results turned out badly, driving me to change from being my only god to pursuing the real God. When I asked for His forgiveness and help, I received both. This allowed me to awaken each morning fresh and forgiven, as opposed to picking up the load of all the mistakes in my life and carrying them with me every step I would take. This weight had destroyed my body and health. But without this load, I was given all I needed. The God Drops were the reward. I have never written a God Drop or a book; I provide the fingers for typing and the mind through which He communicates. Nothing more. I believe the Drops were to help me clean up my life and to share with you, dear reader.

There are many books on how to develop the Presence of God, but Brother Lawrence's letters (*The Practice of the Presence of God the Best Rule of a Holy Life* and *The Practice of the Presence of God with Spiritual Maxims*, both available on Amazon and Kindle) are where I went to learn some of the methods. When I met Brother Lawrence in his letters, I came to know the Presence of God, his life's obsession. His writing taught me that there is no intellectual way to God, only a feeling way. I have found God to have an almost inaudible voice. I want to stress again how soft the voice of God is and how dogged He is at pursuing us. I hope you, the reader, are seeing the way God stayed with me and directed me to where I am today.

God excels in pursuit. I felt His pursuit from my birth until the present. I found I couldn't resist His pursuit and the feeling of His momentary Presence. He continues to lead me back to Him time after time; however, there is never any demand, only a feeling of oneness. At this moment in time, I believe staying in the Presence of God all the time cures everything and feels wonderful. God is all there is now, all there has ever been, and all there will ever be. And He is you and I.

God abhors all distance from us; we were created by Him to be his companions all the time. We are His voice and His actions on this plane of life. If we do not function in this capacity, He is quiet and inactive. He designed this world and allowed love to be the builder of everything, pulling everything together by abolishing all distance from Him. He is not the center of all there is; He *is* all there is. Because of free will, we were allowed to choose whether to spend time with Him or not; however, He will pursue us every minute we live. He will never give up.

God, in my mind, is the singularity in our universe. He is all there is, and He is totally good. However, believing this presents a great problem. If there is only one power in the universe, and it is good, how do we account for evil? All my life, I have been taught about the devil and his power for evil. He is a fallen angel who decided to sponsor evil. If the universe is infinitely good, how can there be an organized power for evil? The more I have looked at free will and the opportunity to choose the absence of God, the more I have understood that this situation might result in more evil than having an organized power for evil. The absence of God and free will would be disastrous. I am afraid this is the situation. We, as man, have the power to be completely evil with no rules in the absence of God. History teaches that some people have become totally evil, which was their choice.

We, as people, have the choice and the responsibility to be totally good or totally bad. Without responsibility, we will make the wrong choice, which is another reason to pursue God with the same fervor as He pursues us. To reject the greatest gift God has given us can be turned into the greatest evil ever created.

If, however, we accept the gift of His association, we will be led to do only good, where all will prosper and find happiness. Again, we meet responsibility and free will. God has already given us all He has to give; the ball is now in our court.

What we decide makes no difference; He will still pursue us. He has already deigned that all roads lead to Him. It is just easier and quicker for us to turn to Him early and stop the chase.

What does matter is that all of us search and find our own path to Him. Without our path, we will be wandering in the desert with no compass or beacon. For forty years I have flown airplanes in the West Texas desert, and without an electrical beacon, compass, or line of sight, there is no way out. The land all looks the same, and all of it is dangerous to be on foot in. The Beacon has been provided; we just have to ask to see it.

My Inadequacies in Writing This Book

I DO NOT FEEL ADEQUATE TO WRITE A DO-IT-YOURSELF BOOK ABOUT FINDING and building a relationship with the infinite Singularity. However, without some suggestions for the reader about how to experience the Presence of God, this book would be incomplete. Since I know only my own path to God, I will draw on my experiences from my own life. I may have been lucky in that my life had reached a point where it would no longer function without change. So with no choice, except to die or change, I became fully open-minded about everything spiritual. With total focus on which way to go, I looked at everything I could find. I found the Bible and tore into it, but I found more confusion than answers. I then discovered Bible interpreters, which were truly godsends. I found New Age doctrines, but they left out Christ. At this point, I found my early life experience with a fundamental religion was really getting in my way.

My tiny relationship with God was now beginning to lead the way. I found religious counselors, who opened doors to options. I had never been given options about spirituality before, which seems stupid now. With these new thoughts and trust in God that I was on the right road, I let God show the way through the minefields of information and misinformation. He showed me what you are now reading.

This search has consumed forty years of my life and is just getting started to where I am going. To me now, any thought about the Divine is to be studied in detail, and I have found parts of all of the new knowledge that fit me. After all, God is infinite and eternal. Who am I to put any limits or restrictions on Him or what He believes? All thought that is founded on love and in God adds to me as a child of the one God. It's made me a better person. I'm more loving, more caring, and more accepting. I have no idea where this search will end, but I do know it is the one journey I have never tired of. We are no different, you and I, and we are all on the same road of discovery. I have discovered this road moves only forward and never turns back on itself. The light leads the way, so, when in doubt, I swim for the light.

The swim for the light comes from my learning to swim. I was taught that when underwater and lost, I didn't have to drown; instead, I could swim for the light. I have always found God in the light, and that light is God's presence in the present, the only place God lives.

We may live eternally, but I guarantee we will only experience the present because I have already lived seventy-nine years, and all I have ever known is this present millisecond. I think we need to understand that God plays no tricks on us. What we see is what we get.

Another thing that needs saying is that at your birth and at my birth, the most excited being there was God. He created you and me to fill the companion slots you and I alone can fill. He has waited just for you and me.

Experiencing the Presence of God

My biggest fear early in the morning is
the blankness of the paper staring at me.
"Blank" neither stimulates me nor stands for anything;
so quickly, I have to write one word
to spoil the page.
Next, I reenter my safe place, which I do by saying,
"I am one with the Presence of God,
and thank you, God, for being One with me."
Then, I enter this present moment,
or better, this present millisecond,
and all other thoughts are culled.
Next, I lean back and see the paper as a vacuum,
knowing that nature abhors a vacuum, and I wait.
As the ideas start, I just write them.
This is why, after writing late into the night,
I can't wait in the morning to see what I have written.

Once I have centered my mind on the Presence,
I have to ask for what I need.
If I am writing, I ask for ideas.
If I am anxious, I request His infinite peace
and close my eyes and picture in my mind the
flow of His peace covering my entire being.

The Presence never controls or dominates my mind.
He appears to me as a cherished guest.

There is such a connection between
the present and the Presence of God
that I once thought they were the same.
I learned God is waiting
in the present for me to come in.
God is always wherever I am,
but I have to *ask* for the meeting.

Of all my relationships, this one with the Presence
has become my favorite.
I now find myself feeling that any time not in
the Presence is wasted.
I function at a higher and more honorable level
when in His company.

What joy I have had spending time with
The Presence of God!

Living in the Presence

In my case, all ideas about the nature and
personality of God were learned at a very early age,
when I was not in a mature enough place
to be analyzing God or the Deity.
Today, after *much* study and thought,
I see how small and scary my idea of God was.
Once I started "messing" with the Presence,
my ideas changed dramatically.
The size of God became infinite.
His total personality changed to love and compassion.
My ideas of selfishness changed to a realization
that all He had made was just for you and me.
His supply for us is infinite—no limits;
it has already been given to us.

My relationship with the Trinity now
is personal and one-on-one.
Gone is any distance from Them.
They become closer than any other relationship—
the one totally safe place in my life.
The Trinity has become nothing to fear, but, instead,
with the Trinity is where I want to spend all my time,
enjoying Their love and peace.

They now are the first place I turn for answers.
When any questions about life or relationships occur,
I go to the Presence and ask for what I need,
and then I wait.
A better answer than mine comes to me,

an answer that is always better than I ever could have conceived.
The comfort They supply becomes so informal
that I am always thinking about Them as my best friends.
This idea is a little intimidating to me in that
They are my Lord and Savior.
Even though I am hesitant to keep the informality,
it appears.
If it were not what They wanted,
this transformation would not have happened.

Today it is my privilege
to honor and worship Them in
the pleasantness of Their comfort.

I don't believe a God Drop has to materialize in one heartbeat. Some of mine have occurred over a long period. Maybe, if I were smarter, they would have occurred sooner. Also, some Drops appear to be the work of us as people, without God being present. But living in the Presence makes everything a God Drop, doesn't it, no matter where the idea originated?

Now follow God Drops and a bunch of wisdom learned by
doing it *all wrong* the first time.

These God Drops, if they stay in my own head,
are of no value to anyone.
Written, they are released to live
their own lives.

Spirit

I have a feeling that there is another "me"
that is spirit.
This me will probably be the eternal me;
if this is so, I need to learn all I can
about
the spiritual me.

During my life, I believe this spiritual me has
healed and cared for me.
When I could not or would not take care of myself,
it did that for me.
It may have been the angel that has ridden
my shoulder, whispering,
"Not that way."
The main reason I can't always hear it may be
it is sitting in the middle of my brain, originating
many of my thoughts.
Since all thoughts come from the brain,
I cannot distinguish the angel's thoughts from my thoughts.

I have lived my whole life with the physical me,
but time is passing.
I have only tasted a spiritual life,
but if there is a change in my future,
the Presence will lead me into
the new life.

The word "spirit" in other languages
is wind, air, and vapor.
So it has no physical body and makes little noise.
This really hinders a
one-on-one relationship.

The spiritual me is very quiet, like God.
It is not pushy or loud like the physical me.
It does not need or beg for anything,
nor will it grow old.

The spiritual me was given the first seat
at the conference table of me.
I think it leads with presence, not bluster.
I hope its intelligence leads the meetings.

The spirit evidently really cares for me
because as many times as my life has tried to kill me,
without the spirit, I wouldn't be here.

Love

Love is the conductor of the
eternal symphony of me.

My granddaughter's love wrapped around me this morning,
carrying me to the most wonderful tea party.

Love is not timid or shy.
It drives me to repair relationships and
to build more bridges to new friends.

Love obliterates all negative emotions and unifies all things.

Love is another word for *perfection*.

Love is showing me how much there is to love and giving me
the tools to make it happen.

Love has always hovered over me, guiding all I have done.

Without love there is nothing at all
because love is the master builder of the universe.
That is why God is love.

I thought love was what I would receive.
Now I know love is also
what I am to give away.

This is to be only one day in the eternal life of love.

Love may be the eternal me.

I can only truly know you if you want and allow me to,
and if you trust me.

Trust is the basis of how much we give to each other.

If I truly trusted everyone and led with that trust,
would the love I find be
materially more or less than any hurt?
I must go ahead and love anyway.

I can know and love you only if I give myself totally to you.

It has been said, "With love, a child is born.
Without love, a child dies."

Get off your own crooked path,
and let love show the way.

True love will free all that I love. If I *need* someone,
I will try to control him or her.
Love builds everything; it then wraps it
with itself and gives itself away.

Love is recognition of anything that gives and receives love.
If my heart rate changes,
I am most likely in the presence of love.

I think I know a lot about love. How is that possible?
Love is not an object that can be analyzed.
At best, it is a feeling leaving me and traveling
to the object of my love.
It can also be my receiving love from other sources.
Is love just a double-lane road with love itself being the only way?

As love leaves and comes back,
it is diminishing the distance
because it is attempting to eliminate everything
except oneness.

The Bible tells me, "God is love."
If, when I feel love, am I not
already in the Presence of God?

God may be the only being that desires no distance.

In my quest to be more loving,
I am giving up my need for distance from everyone.
Quite often, my love goes up a notch when I
hold anything I love in both of my hands.

What would happen if, when we meet each other,
we all would lead with love?
What would happen if the only agenda were love?

Love is another word for courage.
It overwhelms all the self-preservation instincts
of two young people as they give themselves away to each other.
Only love could prepare a young person
to die for family or country.

Love is the only way a young mother can give
one hundred percent
of herself away to her child.

Love is the magic pill that brings
dead relationships back to life.

There is no way to confine love;
it will break into or out of any life,
no matter the age or the barriers.

There is no way to know even a small amount about love
and not know that God is pursuing us.

Having other people in my life,
I still need touch and smiles of recognition.

It may not be the absence of people we hate;
it may be the absence of love.

Love's glue is the absence of distance.

Love is the only thing I never tire of.

If God is love, and I believe He is,
we can't even begin to comprehend
the depth of His love for us.

Fear

I do not *have* to be fearful;
I *choose* to be fearful.

When I give myself totally to God,
fear unravels.

In the coldness of overwhelming fear,
I choose to surrender or
"put on the full armor of God" and stare it down.

When darkness comes and fear
is driving me into the ground,
I fall back on my forty years of flying.
I retract the gear and continue to fly.
With all my talents required in the flying,
I gain the time and talent
needed to defeat the darkness.

If I weigh only one hundred ten pounds,
and if my God is great and gives me the aim of David,
the fear giant is slain.

Fear (or Death) walked around my bed last night,
and I have never been that cold.
Shaking all over, I mentally
put on the armor of God.
Fear vanished
and was replaced by a very good night's sleep.

Fear, you will never be my friend,
and I am learning the chinks in your armor.

Fear cannot back up its bluster.

When facing the fear bully,
cold sweats and shortness of breath drain away
as I call on my God.

Fear, I know your old evil twin, Anger, very well.
You two have been the giant cancers in my life,
and I love watching you both
shrink and die.

Anger

When I'm angry, a black curtain drops over my brain,
and it sees nothing that is real or correct.

When I decide to become angry, I turn into a base person—
a person I don't like.

My anger comes with volume
but not control.

For a great deal of my life,
anger was my associate,
but it is no longer welcome.

When I was addicted to adrenalin,
I felt almost constant anger.

I thought I enjoyed anger,
but like a snake,
it was slowly swallowing me.

Anger precedes many very poor decisions.

I don't understand the need for anger.
Perhaps my ancestors had very cruel and dangerous enemies
and few weapons.

Falling under the influence of anger far exceeds
the danger of all other addictions
because it damages those around us.

Anger is a poor guest,
and it offers no positive reward for
giving it a home.

The other day, anger called my name,
but now it has to catch me before it can move in.

I was told to count to ten and anger would dissipate;
I could have counted to ten thousand and not changed it.
What I did was stopped giving anger a place to live
and mentally weaned myself from it.

Hatred

I have had no need for hatred;
I have had enough anger to destroy the world
without hatred.

I am smart enough to realize that
hatred is an integral part of many people's lives.
It seemed to me that hatred was what
got them up in the morning and
put them to sleep after dark.
I always wondered,
Did they hate themselves or the person they held
in the sights of their hatred?

To me, hatred is a copout.
If I hate someone enough,
I don't have to change myself.
After all, everything that is wrong is *their* fault
and could not possibly be mine.

All time spent enjoying hatred diminishes
my relationship with the Divine
and with other people.
Hatred will always be stopped dead in its tracks
by love and forgiveness.

Hatred turns the boundaries of a life inward,
diminishing life's size.

Forgiveness

Forgiveness costs nothing,
and it is the reclaimer of lost friends.

I have found forgivingness is the way
to cure most of my ailments.

Any day is a good day
when I am armed with forgiveness.

When forgiveness is added to any fight,
the fight will dissipate.

Forgiveness is one of life's principal
stain removers.

Yesterday's forgiveness
is today's cherished action.

I believe it is impossible for me
to live one full day without allowing
something or someone to hurt me.
Therefore,
forgiveness is essential.

Hurt is the most painful of wounds and has only one remedy:
forgiveness.
The one person I have to forgive daily is myself.
Yes, I can hurt myself more than anyone else
by saying stupid things to myself.
But what injures me even more
is hurting other people.

Life

I now think life would have been easier to live
if we had done it backward.
Why did I have to start life as unlearned as I was?

Uncontrolled ambition and sex are like
unbroken animals, crazy and wild;
but when they are broken to ride, they will
carry us faster than the wind.
However, ambition and sex, when in charge, do not know
truth, love, or morality.
These truths we must use as their reins
because they are no more than unbridled desires.
Each has a place of honor in our lives,
but each has to be controlled early, or disaster occurs.
Neither ambition nor sex can be placed in charge of any life
without creating many problems.
Early in my life, I completely misunderstood these two forces.
Unhealthy ambition drove me hard to
become more than I thought I was.
While sex's main direction is the procreation of the species,
sex was such a joy that I thought for a
while it would be my whole life.
Then by observation and good coaching,
I learned that these two forces walked
a knife's edge because each possessed an awesome strength.
They were either good or bad—all the time.
They both had to be bridled, directed, and kept on an honorable path.

Playing with either one without respecting its
power for evil as well as for good
is like going to bed with a rattlesnake whose mouth
has been sewn together with thin cotton thread.
In time we too will be snake-bit.

As my maturity evolves,
I will take responsibility for all my actions.
I truly own my life and can enjoy or destroy it.
It is all up to me—no one else.

I came here with all I need to build
the perfect life of being me.

I quite often fall short of my intended goals.
So do I quit trying, or do I use what I have learned to start
the next project farther up the road toward the new goal?

Goals are a master compass for life.
They show where I am located
and where I am going.

I allowed myself to use anger and pride to construct
a giant hole I could not climb out of.
I was then led to weave a rope of forgiveness and love,
and the rope pulled me to level ground.

Life is much more than a series of days.
The days come blank, but, when filled with our emotions and actions,
those days begin to shimmer and dance with life.

If I keep life fluid and flexible, it blends and
wraps around me like a warm blanket.

I keep life talking to me because, with good communication,
we may not kill each other.

Trust should be given with great care
because when it is broken,
it almost destroys the giver.

The young hate to make contracts;
but the old live by contracts,
which are nothing more than
commitments.

A smile costs nothing and means *so* much.

I see in this day what I believe I am.

Could I see more without eyes?
No, but I might *be* more.
Eyes, as wonderful as they are,
often fill me with many distractions.

As a child, I often thought I was special.
As an adult, I know I am special to God.

As a child, I wanted money and more size.
As an adult, I want love and a smaller size.

When will I start thinking of other people
more than I think of myself?
Never, unless I work at love and forgiveness.

An open door is happy and inviting.
Close it, and I am excluded.

Does it make me more human to love my dog,
or more dog to love other humans?

I used to love riding horses, but I don't miss riding.
It is like so many other things in my life that I ended
in order to try something new.

A smile makes anyone prettier and more interesting.

A frown always depresses me and makes me feel guilty.

As a child, I thought everyone had
an angry face and was judging me.
As an adult, I found that if I changed my fear of people
into love for them,
all the faces could be changed into smiling faces that love me.

As a child, when I was alone,
I would hide in the dark.
As an adult, I worked at relationships
that buffered me from
being alone and in the dark.

Watching birds is more than a pastime;
it is a study of beauty in motion.

All my life, I have wanted to know who or what I am.
Now I know I have always been the total me;
however, it was up to me to recognize,
claim, and live what I already was.

As I have walked the path of life,
the thorns have proven to be more important
than the smooth pavement.

I don't think I have ever really *known* another person—
not even my parents or my sister.
Kay, after fifty-five years of marriage,
is the closest I've come to knowing someone, but,
thank God, I still only know her partially because
learning even more of her is the joy of my life.

I hate to eat by myself, so I started phoning
all my friends who are still alive.
He was busy.

Life travels or rolls on, and I have decided my best option,
sometimes, is to get out of its way.

Smiles are beautiful and contagious.

With all mental roads leading to the Divine, it is easier for me
to get on the road and let it take me there.

Acquired knowledge is worthless until I believe it
and incorporate it into my being.

Smiles turn upward, and frowns turn downward.
For me, upward is flying into a semi-cloudy sky,
punching between the white piles of moisture,
and feeling the G's of flight.
Downward is bending over and pulling weeds.

I don't believe we ever stopped playing in the sandbox.
After all, that is where we learned
how to use imagination and how to get along
with the neighborhood kids.
In some cases, a sandbox is where we learned to fight
and how to say we were sorry.
We are still in the same sand, but I am afraid we do not hold
the other players or games in the
same esteem as we did as children.
We have replaced spontaneity with rules and scorekeeping.

I always thought girls knew more about life than I did.
Girls thought we boys had all the answers.
So now we understand why the divorce rate is so high.

The river of my youth was free and cool.
As I played in the water, I was being cleaned and filled with energy
because of my love for the river.
The next swimmer, I am sure, saw it differently.

Is the human heart a muscle-driven pump
that only delivers blood to all my body?
Literature would lead me to believe that
it is also the seat of my emotions.
I would think the brain
would be the center of emotions.
However, I do know that "crying my
heart out" seems more plausible
than "crying my brain out."

Is my whole world only what I see or nothing?
If it is different to each of us,
does the world even exist?

I believe the physical world that I know and love
is no more than my view of life
and satisfaction with myself.

I need to develop myself as the person
who satisfies me first.
Without satisfaction with myself,
I am in a terrible place.

I accomplish little without being driven
by some unseen force.
Hasn't it always been the Divine
showing me the route?

I am extremely messy; I love being messy.
It would take ten people to "less mess" my world.

We live in a small house;
however, I only live in ten percent of it.
All I need is one room with a bath,
but then it might not be large enough
for all my mess and me.

Success seems multidimensional.
Seldom do I see a person being successful
in only one area of life.

I think I will remain a proxy Christian in any
church service starting before dawn.

I used to be a "Clint Eastwood Christian" because
getting even was all I thought about.

This millisecond of eternity is all
I will ever experience and *own!*

I, like my dogs, don't know whether to run
or hide when the big dogs bark.

When my dog, Maddie, comes to me for petting,
is it my petting her, or her petting me?

Life will always be my greatest gift.
There is no way to give enough thanks
for just starting my heart and brain.
I hope God, after creating me,
looked at me and was proud;
and today I pray He is looking at me
and still feeling pride.

All of us want to be told we did something right.
This need for recognition
is normal and needed. However, when the normal
turns into an inexhaustible need for compliments,
we have to change or go crazy.
I found early on if I did not receive what I needed,
I would change groups
until I found a source for what I was looking for.
I was to learn later that
the most important person to brag on and thank me
for my efforts was myself.
A word of praise from myself became almost as important as
a word of praise from my father.

The gift of life carries many responsibilities,
but the largest is the gift to reproduce.
I am afraid for many years I got reproduction
and hormones confused.
Today, as I look at my family, I am so proud and
cannot give enough thanks for this one gift.

I can focus now much better than I could when I was young.
I now have to stay in the present while driving
because if I am
thinking about this book and driving,
I can run several other cars off the road.

If I could just live all my life in the present,
most of my problems would never occur.

I am now faced with the same dilemma my ancestors were.
How can I leave any part of my experiences
with my family and friends?
Just like the people before me,
I will take what I have learned to my grave
and leave all those who follow the same opportunity I had,
which is to live life their way, with little or no instruction.
They, like me, have to take responsibility for their own lives.

Are we all so locked into our own minds and ideas
that we look at all other ideas as trivial?

Is the sound of my own voice so important to me
that I no longer appreciate any other voice?
Perhaps, if I decide to enjoy the sounds of the day,
I may just hear celestial sounds
from the people surrounding me.

Has our contempt for the world reached such a point that
we cannot appreciate anything?
It may be time to study the night sky
and really come to grips with how small
and insignificant we really are.
Let's take a step backward and just say thanks for this day
and hope for tomorrow.

Light is synonymous with life.
As a child, I couldn't wait for daylight when play started.

Darkness stopped my playing as a child
and started my playing as an adult.

Light interferes with hiding anything,
but it also points the way back to where
I hid something in the dark.

I can't read your mind, nor can you read mine.
I must ask you, and you have to ask me,
for what you want or need.
This must be love's first conversation.
It is insane for you to think you know what I am thinking,
or for me to know what you are thinking;
we would both be wholly inaccurate.
Relationships work so much better if we just learn to ask
the other party for what we need or want.

Life has so many magical places to take us.
There will always be more to learn
and see than we can handle.
Life is all so easy.
But we can mess up by not living life
in the proper order.
If, however, we do mess up,
we can thank God for the experience
and swim for the light,
just like nothing wrong ever happened.

Life has always been about the enthusiasm we have
for the game and the way we play it.
Do we stop the football carrier coming through the line
head-on, or do we glance off to get
him from behind?
Do we play hurt or find a spot on the bench?
When the temperature is zero,
do we run out on the field
as if it were seventy-two degrees?
Do we get up from a good block, which put us on the ground,
and pat the giver on the back?
Can we walk off the field at the end of the
game, knowing we gave all we had,
that nothing else is left; all we had went into the game.
Can we look up at the stands and know we represented
all of the fans with all we had?
If we can do all of that,
we have done it right and not taken the easy way out.

Without God, life is mostly a highly competitive endeavor.

My self-preservation drive is not because
this life is all there is.
Rather, I want to have the time to get this life right.

As a child, everything was new and possible.
Why did I forget that?

Life is the use of time given me at birth.
It is easy to think it will stop when I die.
I choose the harder route of believing that life continues,
but in a different form.
Life and I were created by Something more than chance;
and now that we have united,
life and I will not cease.
If this is not true, why did God go to the trouble
of creating my life at all in the first place?

Life is not critical of my actions.
Each day, I get to start forgiven and fresh.

Learning

Education, for those who can achieve it,
is wonderful, but
if you give observation the same
focus as you give education,
then observation of any day
anywhere in the world is
the greatest way to learn;
but first we have to recognize that truth.

I attended the university strictly
to learn how to become rich.
What I really found was
an infinite universe, filled with golden ideas,
which means more to me than
all the gold on this planet.

I so hope that the hereafter is
an infinite library,
and I won't need glasses.

Often I think light and learning are the same.
I do know they have to work together.

Why did I ever waste time
quarrelling over an idea
when there are so many new ideas
to learn that don't require
an argument?

I have not yet learned to see all people as friends.
I also don't see all ideas as friends.

Learning is my constant need—
peeling away the static of interference
and searching out the heart of an idea.

Days were created for learning.
We get to dig in the pile of chaos
and extract
the chunks of knowledge.

I now recognize why I started life
so unlearned.
If there were nothing to learn,
why was I ever here?

I was given boredom to lead me
back to my reason for living,
which is learning.

Ideas are layers of information
gathered by observation
with a heart of truth.

New ideas fill my days with
golden nuggets of truth.

Thank God I live in a constant swirl of ideas
and my joy is to capture some of them.

All the effort of learning new ideas is
worthwhile because they never decay and
have given me much comfort
when I am alone.

Truth is not static.
It can grow with more knowledge
and change with sound arguments.
Truth is a treasure to be proud of
and enjoy.

I hated school and learning as a child.
Now there is not enough time for learning
all I crave to know.

After death, I pray that
all emphasis is on learning
and the teachers are
patient and brilliant.

Mind

Quite often a bigger mind
creates bigger struggles.

My mind is the total me,
and it creates what I believe I am.

I don't live where I reside.
I am, and live in, my mind.
My consciousness is me.

My mind trains me and
shows me how to train it.

My brain is not my mind.
My brain is something one can
take out and hold.
My mind is infinite,
and I can't see it or hold it;
I only know and feel it.

Even if my mind is infinite,
I get to decide how much of it I recognize and use.

I am beginning to wonder,
Is my mind a remote station to
the eternal and infinite Mind?
If it is not,
my mind is not nearly large enough.

Problems

Thank God, the world itself has no problems.
We, on the other hand, coined the word *problem*
to be the excuse for not being able to crawl out
of the cauldron of life and
swim for the light.

The reason no single person can solve
all problems is simple:
solving problems is why we were all put here.

Problems are easy to find.
Solutions are hidden under many layers
of information.

Problems are to be avoided by most,
but to the next generation of wealthy people,
they are tirelessly hunted
because hidden somewhere
in the problem is always
the solution.

Large problems are like a flat tire—
only flat on one side.
A small problem may sometimes take
a lifetime to resolve.

Worry

Worry has taken much of my time.
Worry does not solve anything,
and time is too valuable to waste while
running in a blind alley of worry.

Making a plan and then working on the plan
can solve all worries.
Lying in bed, wet with sweat and rolling in the covers,
never solved anything for me.
It did make me very sleepy the next day.

What works for me is dissecting my
problems on a legal pad,
putting the problems in one column
and all the solutions in another column,
and then getting a good night's sleep.

Problems are much smaller in the daylight,
and worry seems, somehow, to go away.

I enjoyed good health when I was young.
My mind created most of my health issues.
Good medicine and disciplined thinking
solved them.

All time spent not in the present
is inviting worry to come in.
When worry first comes to me,
I immediately mentally go to the present
and forget worry.

Fatigue

Yesterday I set a goal for my bicycle ride
that was beyond my ability,
and my muscles started shutting down.
A dear friend drove up,
and three minutes of his and my laughter refreshed me
more than thirty minutes of rest.

Often my fatigue is the product of boredom,
not exercise.

I can slow fatigue by slowing my pace.

Endurance tops speed.

If I am eternal,
there is no need to hurry.

I am finding life is an endurance activity.
Comfort falls away replaced by burning, aching muscles.
As the pain becomes unbearable,
a calm falls over my body,
and I acquire a pace that appears automatic,

which is known to runners as a second wind
or a runner's high.
This calm is where great things happen.
The calm brings clarity of thought and feelings that
may not be of this body or of this world.
This runner's high may be almost spiritual.

Reality

Reality is quite often harder and more tiring
than make-believe.
Make-believe is like a handful of sand leaking through
the fingers on a very windy day.
The wind is doing the work,
and the sand is riding the wind into oblivion.

Reality and freedom give only one thing:
opportunity.

Reality rides on wheels of perspiration.

Reality says I have no rights to anything I didn't first build.
Fantasy says I am going to sit in this chair,
and those who are working
are going to share their results with me.

Reality says no matter how much I own or control,
I will live until I die.
I will be remembered for no more than
one, maybe two, generations.

Days

At age five, walking home on a warm March day from a
friend's house, I saw a lone flower in a pasture.
I picked it and carried it home to my mother.
On the long trip home, the flower fell apart,
and all I had left when I got there were the stem and seedpod.
Crying, I offered the remainder to my mother.
She looked at the stem and pod.
She grabbed me and hugged me and said,
"I thank you so very much.
This flower is the first flower of spring and
the only first flower I have ever received as a gift."
She just held and kissed me.

How magnificent was this day.
It gave all it had just for me
and then winked at me at sunset.

This day may be all I have.
If I knew I were dying today,
should I change what I'm doing, or should
I just do what I had already planned?

This day was a complete gift.
Even if I worked, I worked *with* it, not *for* it.

I can't change the content of this day,
but maybe I can move it around some.

Yesterday is gone,
and we are not quite sure about tomorrow.

I can predict tomorrow by looking at today.
They both start with so much promise.
Where they go is always up to me.

I let today take its own path.
When I got out of the way,
both the day and I were
very successful.

The blueness of the sky and the brilliance
of the sun soothe and warm my day.
Perfection and beauty
are always close to my hands and eyes.

Birds singing on a spring morning make
my heart younger and my day freer.

The day walked in this morning, carrying its light.
Or did the light blast a hole in the darkness
this morning, creating this day?

A day is the theater I live in.
It comes to me blank, and I get to play with filling it all in.
It can be all drab or all color;
it can smell fragrant or repulsive.
It matters not to the day;
after all, it is only the stage.
We are the actors. We are the play.
The curtain will open, and the act goes on
until the final curtain.
The day is unconcerned with whether we were good or bad.
We will suffer or rejoice in our performance
only if we choose to.

The day came early, before I was ready.
I took the day for granted and made no preparation.
At best, I will receive about 30,000 days,
which seems like a lot,
but I have already used 27,270 days.
I wish I had not wasted
even one.

Of all the days I have lived, I will choose
this one, *today*. It is the only day I own now,
and four hundred billion years
of experimentation and genetics have been
invested in this one day.

The universe has an enormous investment in this day,
and I received it for free.

What a wonderful day this is.
There is a roaring wind blowing outside, and it is very cold,
but I am inside.
I am so fortunate that I was given
a comfortable chair and a fireplace.
The warm dog in my lap and I have only
one responsibility to this day—
a nap in this chair.

I do not want to be responsible today;
I don't want to work either.
I can be lazy
and occasionally need something to push me.

The day slipped into my sleeping bag last night,
awakened me at first light, and promised nothing
but her constant attention to me until it was time
for me to sleep once again.
She kept that promise in spades.
A day is a lady that can be trusted.

Why do I feel such apprehension some days?
It has to be my inability to trust
that I am loved and guarded.

My all-time best day was the day I realized God wanted
a relationship with me more than I wanted one with Him.
If this were not so, it would be impossible to have a relationship
with the infinite and eternal.

With two female dogs and Kay in the family,
we share so much love and trust that
each day is
like Christmas morning.

This day lighted up a howling wind, tearing apart
the small, gray clouds;
each was reduced to a wispy, dry, ragged, fast-moving mirage.
Needing rain so badly, I turned away in disgust,
almost missing what I was here to see.
There were five golden, ever-so-bright columns holding up
the ragged mess of wind and cloud.
No rain today, but instead, the most beautiful
display of sunlight shafts,
reminding me how much
God loves His desert.

This was a great day;
I got to visit with friends,
eat a nice lunch, and take a nap.
I also got to write for four hours.
Was it wasted,
or did I help someone more than me?

The day kicked me out of bed before I was ready.
Why am I not consulted before the day
thrusts me from unconscious to conscious?
On some days,
Unconscious is just better.

How could anyone have this very day without knowing
that there is nothing on earth that could replace
what we have already received for free?

Ah, what a day. "The possibilities!"

Night

The wonder of this night
makes this day complete.

Is the night sky's blackness just a background,
or is it as important as the stars?
I am afraid that without the black
we could not see the brilliance.

This moonless night is Mother Nature's
earned rest
before her greatest creation—
tomorrow.

I have never been able to get the day
to wrap around me as the cold blackness of a moonless night does.
But I also have never been able to trust a night
as much as I can trust a day.

Rights

It is true we were given
all the gifts in the universe
with basically no restrictions.
To be given so much freedom
with no instructions
had to be a gift from God.
No person I have met
would have ever done such a thing.

I had great parents who tried
to bring me up to speed
on what to do and what not to do
in order to have a happy life.
After leaving home, I discovered there are
literally no limits on us, other than having
to obey some laws.

Most of us talked to our buddies about
how to have the most fun,
with little or no thought
about living the accepted way.
After all, we thought we were
totally bulletproof
and nothing could hurt us.
After a long time, we began to connect the
painful results we were feeling
with certain poor decisions we had made.

I finally realized how long it took for me
to understand that I had been given
the wheel to drive my life at birth.
This understanding, no matter how long
in incubation, revolutionized my life.

Once I began to drive my life,
so much information came together,
and my goals changed
one hundred eighty degrees.
Now, I cannot learn enough about life
and how to live it better.

When I first got drafted into the army,
they gave me a code of conduct document
that pointed out what life skills the army wanted
and what the punishments were for not keeping
their code of conduct.
The last forty years of my life have been spent
building *my* code of conduct for *now*.

Control

Control of the normal civilian population
is a great deal like herding cats or quail.
Normally, any type of unagreed-to control
will result in an organized group fighting everything
that the controller wants done.

Control of almost any type goes against
the normal life of the controlled.
Left alone, most people want and will die
for freedom, not control.

Without exception, all who have tried
controlling large populations have failed.
Normally, the would-be controller
dies in the end also.

The only successful control
is self-control.

Domination

Control can't exist without
domination.

Domination can't exist with
freedom or love.

Domination requires the physical
slavery of the dominated.

Domination is the end game
of greed.

Lack of responsibility is
the fertile soil that produces
control and domination.

Domination walks the streets
hunting and capturing the weak.

Domination often leads to
war of some type.

Freedom

Freedom has no limits,
but slavery is nothing but limits.

Freedom is quiet and gives its host
the opposite of fear and domination.

Freedom is normally the child
of sacrifice.

Freedom is a gift that must
be protected.

Freedom is often bought and lost
at the end of a gun.

Freedom will be lost no other way except
through neglect
and failure to protect it.

When freedom is lost,
it will not be regained for several generations.

The price of freedom is the death
and sacrifice for many
who probably never knew freedom,
but only dreamed of it.

Freedom is the opposite of control.

Freedom lives only in the midst of
total responsibility.

Life without freedom is another concept
of hell.

Freedom is so valuable
we should rise to our feet
even to discuss it.

Respect

Respect is never given
until it is earned.

Respect determines
my place in the pecking order.

A person can live most of life
and have gained total respect,
but one bad decision
can destroy it all.

We think when we have earned respect,
it is ours to keep,
but it is not;
it will always rest in the hands of our peers.
Respect, like freedom, has to be
protected and earned
each and every day.

Friends

My friends are the padding
that protects me from
life's hardest blows.

A real friend will
be constructed out of love.

Real friendship leaves little
or no room
for anything except
assistance, fun, and love.

Seeing the smiling face of a friend
has always been my greatest
"upper."

My family was a gift.
My friends, I worked at nurturing.
Now they fill in my weaknesses.

Aloneness

My small house becomes very small
when I am alone.
I am little different from my small dog that
substitutes sleep for life if she is alone.
Is that what I see in nursing homes?
Maybe without human relations,
we die or totally zone out.

My aloneness is driving me
to reconnect to my real life.
My physical self can be fine being a little alone,
but my spiritual self suffers from being alone.
Little except the Divine
can heal aloneness.

I do not feel alone when
I choose to be alone.

Inside a crowd of unknown people,
we are all alone.
When I'm by myself, big cities are
the loneliest places on earth.
Only with other unknown people,
do I want to run away.
By building cities, I am afraid we
have created unacceptable loneliness.

This day I will spend with the Divine
because I am without other people.

I hate to admit this:
churches without people and love
are very lonely places.

Life *alone* would be little
or no life at all.

Broken People

I found a broken couple on the back stoop
of our church several Sundays ago.
They were very old and cold.
I just stood and watched them
without their seeing me.
I could have done many things for them,
but I didn't do anything.
That's not true; I passed the buck
and told the janitor where they were.
He passed the buck and told me
that's where they lived.
Then they walked across the street
and straightened their clothes.
They picked up their sacks and walked off,
shuffling away
in search of a Christian and breakfast.
Who was the most broken?

I found a broken lady
selling newspapers on Sunday,
and now I give her twenty dollars a week.
Is the money for her or for me?

Wrapped in education and comfort I live,
but I am a farmer who maybe is not putting
enough seed back into the ground.

All over town, we have shelters
for broken people,
and we give money to most of them.
Oh, God, is this enough?
I think not.
Please forgive me.

I am just learning what Jesus knew—
all people on this planet are broken.
I so hope my writing leads to
a worldwide effort of shouting,
"We can help this brokenness!"
With God's help,
we can turn to working,
not just watching other people
work and cheering them on.
Let's get in the game ourselves
and not sit on the bench.

Roads

Roads have always stood for freedom.
The road, with the wind in our hair, will whisk us
to somewhere we have never been.

I believe I always preferred the trip more than the destination.
To me, the destination seemed to be like where I lived,
but the road was always new.
What wonder lives around the next bend?

The beauty of a road is that it never
turns back on itself.
It only moves forward and
takes me to new worlds.

The surface of the road is like life.
It is smooth or rough, dusty or clean.
Like life, I am being taken somewhere else,
hoping for something better.

The road starts and ends, and has magic all along the way.
It is a never-ending "guess what."

Roads shadowed with trees are
the absolute best roads.

Roads going through small
towns with the smell of burning autumn leaves
return me to my youth.

Supply

Supply Comes from the Divine but Depends
on Our Efforts to Enhance It.

I awakened this morning and wrapped myself in the day.
That's when I realized I was immensely wealthy.
I had no more money than the day before,
but I decided what I did have was enough,
so I became immensely wealthy.
With nothing else to do,
I just played with the rest of the day.

Now that I am wealthy,
I have decided no longer to be a seeker
and have become an observer.
Now I just sit and let life dance around me;
occasionally, I feel the urge to applaud but never
to pass judgment or to criticize.

I used to think supply could only be acquired
by knowing the powerful and rich.
Also, accruing an education was a must.
Now I know supply comes from God,
and all I have to do is work, be honest,
and talk to Him on a daily basis.
Then I give Him all the credit and thanks.

To believe that all wealthy individuals received
my portion of wealth is absolutely absurd.
Everything in this universe is infinite;
there is no such thing as my portion or their portion.
No matter how long mankind lives and prospers,
there will be no less supply than when
he first started accruing possessions.

Contacts with other people will always be
just what they are:
friends to enjoy but not to use.
If I can help a friend, my duty is to do just that,
but I am not to take anyone
other than my children and family
to raise and supply with income.

My experience leads me to realize
that having money solves few problems,
but it can create a boatload of them.

I now believe that to receive an infinite gift,
I must also return infinite gratitude.
I wonder whether the amount of gratitude I gave may have
resulted in the amount of good I received.
None of us can muster infinite thanks,
but what I have been able to muster has been enough.

I now believe that first I have to receive God's gift,
claim it, and give thanks for it
before it becomes mine.

I am becoming aware that the only obstacle
between my total supply and me has been myself.
Emerson said, "Let us take our bloated nothingness
out of the path of the divine circuits."
I find it very distressing to admit that
only *I* have limited most of the
abundance I thought I deserved.

Total abundance has always been
a free gift under my name,
but I never went to the front desk to claim it.

I believe most of my prayers have been wrong.
I was always asking for something I thought I needed.
Now I believe everything was given to me at birth;
however, I *must claim* it to receive it.
The Divine, listening to me and smiling, said,
"I should have created this one smarter."

When I was young, life seemed so easy,
but I was to find a life lived right was so demanding
that few people would pay its price.
Life is just so much easier to half-live than
to stay those extra hours and do it right.

I have known but few wealthy people
who didn't earn most of it after everyone else
had gone home.

Life is always a trade off.
If I want these possessions,
what am I willing to trade for them?
The prize or destination always has a cost.
Our part in the game is to decide,
"Is it worth it?"

Most of us walk through this life, seeing little.
If we see anything at all, it is usually someone else's crumbs,
when we should have been thinking,
"How can I serve other people in a way that does not now exist?"

Service that no one else
is willing to provide to mankind
has generated most of the fortunes.

I may have been fortunate to be born
with few possessions,
so I gave little thought to money.
I had no money, so why worry about it?
To me, money was just a lubricant.
Without it, I had to work much harder,
but with it, things seemed to work easier.

When Kay shattered her femur and was in surgery,
the doctor told me that when the rod was in place
and he started to tighten the tension on the leg,
the twenty-some-odd pieces of bone just knew
where they were supposed to be and went there.
He was amazed at how quickly
the operation was over
because of his not having to place each piece
back in its correct spot.
To me, having the universe's best Physician assisting her doctor
was worth more than money.

If I am too good to do some kinds of work,
I am too good to prosper.

Kay and I were in a McDonald's one morning observing
the sorriest bunch of employees I have ever seen—doing nothing.
One lone Hispanic boy was doing 90 percent of the work.
Kay remarked that she felt sorry for the kid.
I, on the other hand, saw the next restaurant tycoon.
What was obvious to me was that he had figured out how to be
paid to learn the most up-to-date restaurant technology.
His next step will be his own place,
and he will bring all the new ideas to it.

Let's be honest, someone else already owns
what is on the market.
What's wrong with getting a trash-handling job

and coming up with a better way
to handle the world's trash?
I happen to know two brothers who are doing that now,
but first they were trash haulers.
Now they could buy all of us.

If we could all just quit looking at the ground
for loose change,
and look to the sky for the universe,
most of the world's problems could be healed.

Time

To the universe there is no time,
only the present.

Man is the only being who
uses time and also wastes time.

Time holds mankind in a form of slavery.
Man, *not* God, invented time.

To many people, time is God.

Before man invented time,
all things that needed to be done
still got done.

I used to wait for 5:00 p.m. to come
so my real day would start.

In the present second,
99.99 percent of the time,
I have no needs.

I can turn this day into eternity
by watching a clock.

Time slows my production
because the closer I get to a deadline,
the more confused I become.

Eternity will not be blissful
if there is a clock.

I believe we, as people, were designed
to live mostly in the present.
Without the past or future taking
up our time, everything could
work together as one whole.

As I have trained my mind
to stay in the present,
my life has become
materially better.

Infinity

I so hope I don't have to fully
understand infinity
to be one with it.

Because of imagination
an empty box with six walls
is almost infinite.

What is infinity?
Where can I acquire a sack of infinity?
If I could find the infinity store,
would I be able to afford a sack of infinity?

To me, infinity is more
a question of facts
than a statement of facts.

I hope I am more a guest of infinity
than a parasite.

I suspect I have lived in infinity
and not even recognized it.

I had to reach about twenty-five years of age
before I could even think of infinity
without being frightened.
Now I am naive enough to hope that
I am a part of it.

I still love to play "when I grow up."
The idea of the sentence is
infinite.

Aging

As I have aged, my physical body has
deteriorated and slowed.
My mind, on the other hand,
paid no attention and roared ahead in search
of more life and learning.

Aging is more than interesting.
I did not ask for it; it just happened.
It does not seem to apply to anything
except my physical body.

Maybe we are like a butterfly that sloughs off
the package it is born in
to become the beauty it truly is.

Aging is painful and limiting.
Is it just another thorn or rock on the road to maturity?
Both aging and pain are important,
or we would not have them.

I will not give in to age. If it kills me,
I will come back eternally young.

Quitting has not been my style.
So with stooped shoulders and failing eyesight,
I will rise to go another round with the enemy
until I hear the dirt hit the lid of my box.

Age hurts so badly that it is not amusing.
Age's evil army is attacking my old body
and has a map of my weak spots.
Daily attacks are launched against my defenses,
hitting hard at where I am the weakest.
I am rapidly reaching the point that
when I do win, all I can do is limp away
to regroup my old, wrinkled troops.
What I would give for some new troops
that are not as old as I!

I don't want to wait for the hereafter;
I want my youth back now.

Death

Death is either the end to everything or
the start of all there is.

Death seems to apply only to the physical body.
Life, the part of my being I can't see,
appears not to age or incur infirmities.

Birth and death are two parts of the same life.
I really don't remember anything before I was born,
but that does not keep me from feeling there was something before.
I can't see a black hole in the universe,
but that does not mean there is not one.

Going with God is just better than going with chance.
If there is nothing after life, I won't even know it;
but if there is, and I miss it,
I will have made a very poor choice.

All people wish they hadn't drawn a hand
where birth has only one requirement:
death.

You say there is not enough room for all of us
to have eternal life.
I say we, on this planet, are not even a tiny point
on the map of the universe.
All who have ever lived can enjoy eternal life.

Thoughts of death take almost none of my time now.
When I was younger,
I worried and fretted about dying.
Now that the hooded face of death is just around the corner,
my fear of death is giving way to
my desire to know for sure.

When I die,
I will take what I have learned with me.
Without that,
I will not be me.

Death is asking the greatest question ever asked:
"What happens after life?"

Eternity

I have to look to the sky
and see eternity
before I can believe it exists.

I love to think about eternity,
but I would love understanding eternity more
than just pondering it.

If I could find someone who could
explain eternity to me,
wouldn't it take an eternity?

I used to think eternity was too long;
Now I am concerned
it won't be long enough.

Hope

Hope stands in the middle of chaos and directs
the traffic toward peace and order.

Hope is the first place to turn
when darkness invades my life.

Hope has been the beacon sitting on the hill
quietly leading me home.

When the Divine leads,
He leads with hope.

Hope has been my pacifier on many a dark night.

As the cold, dark night wraps itself around me,
chilling me to the bone,
I am all right because I remember my
dented and battered shield:
God's hope.

Hope is the brother to Divine courage
and the father of peace.

Hope, like perseverance,
never tires and moves only forward.

God

If I have just today,
I will spend all of it thanking God
for all He has given me.

Riding horseback at sunrise, on a semi-foggy morning,
will always be to me as good as life gets.
Each time, I felt God had me in His shirt pocket,
allowing me to peer out over the top.

If I have a limited God,
I will live a limited life.

To be one with God means
there is nothing in this universe
that can slow or stop
our progress together.

If I am dressed in the armor of an infinite God,
I can only smile and laugh aloud while looking
at one hundred armed troops marching toward me
swearing an oath to kill me.
God has always loved big odds against Him in a fight.

I am loved and guarded by God.

I am a poor Christian, but, thank God,
I would be a worse atheist.

If God were not infinite love, the
universe would collapse.
Love is the only emotion that builds
and then glues everything together.

Life without God really does not matter.
Only one decision can change it all.
I hated and cursed Him and ran away from Him.
I was my only god for quite some time.
Ten minutes on my knees,
honestly giving my life to Him,
and getting out of His way led to
the best life I have ever known.
This is truly the road home.

I am one with the Presence of God today.
Thank you, God,
for being one with me.

I am just faithful enough to believe God
waited in anticipation of our relationships.
He did it all just for us.

God knows who we are and what we will become,
but because of our free will,
He still grieves or cheers for each of our decisions.

When we punch the ball in the end zone,
God just has to jump out of His seat, yelling,
"That's my child, and I am so proud!"

I believe the happiest being at your birth and at my birth
may have been God.

All roads lead to God,
and, to me, it seems impossible to avoid
going in any direction that does not lead to God.
One really has to take the long way home
to remain an atheist.

Freedom of choice is the divine gift God
placed in me and everyone else;
each one of us must decide how much
of the gift we want to accept.

My first memory was of an imaginary friend
who was almost another me,
except bigger and smarter.
He went everywhere I did and kept me from
being alone when I was by myself.
He never said anything;
I just always pictured him smiling.
But as I grew older, I became so busy
that I didn't keep his relationship.
Now I am working almost around the clock
trying to find him again.

God, being infinite, could not have created me
without giving all of Himself to me at my creation,
But everything He gave me came wrapped in
freedom of choice.

If God, Jesus, and the Holy Spirit can hear
every prayer coming from
this planet at the same time,
it makes sense to me that when I go to heaven
after my death, I will be able to be with the Trinity
any or all of the time by myself
and have Their full attention.

God looks straight through *what* I am
and sees only *who* I am.